D1372949

My First Time

Going to the Dentist

Kate Petty, Lisa Kopper, and Jim Pipe

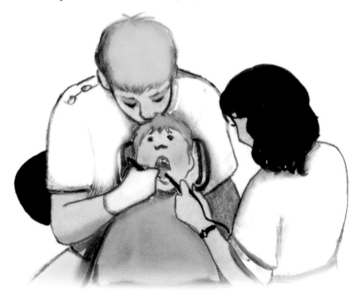

Stargazer Books

© Aladdin Books Ltd 2008

Designed and produced by
Aladdin Books Ltd

First published in 2008
in the United States by
Stargazer Books
c/o The Creative Company
123 South Broad Street
Mankato, Minnesota 56002

Printed in the United States
All rights reserved

Illustrator: Lisa Kopper

Photocredits:
All photos from istockphoto.com.

Library of Congress Cataloging-in-Publication Data

Petty, Kate.
  Going to the dentist / by Kate Petty.
      p. cm. -- (My first time)
  Includes Index.
  ISBN 978-1-59604-158-5 (alk. paper)
   1. Children--Preparation for dental care--Juvenile literature. 1. Title.
RK63.P47 2007
617.6--dc22
                    2007001769

About this book

New experiences can be scary for young children. This series will help them to understand situations they may find themselves in, by explaining in a friendly way what can happen.

This book can be used as a starting point for discussing issues. The questions in some of the boxes ask children about their own experiences.

The stories will also help children to master basic reading skills and learn new vocabulary.

It can help if you read the first sentence to children, and then encourage them to read the rest of the page or story. At the end, try looking through the book again to find where the words in the glossary are used.

Contents

Sam is waiting to see the dentist.
He looks around at all the posters.

Then he watches the fish with Jenny.
When will it be our turn?

4

The dental nurse asks them to come in.
The dentist says hello to Mom and Jenny.

But where is Sam going?
Come back, Sam!

"Who wants to ride in my chair first?
How about you, Sam?
Then Jenny can see what we do."

Sam thinks he'll let Jenny go first.

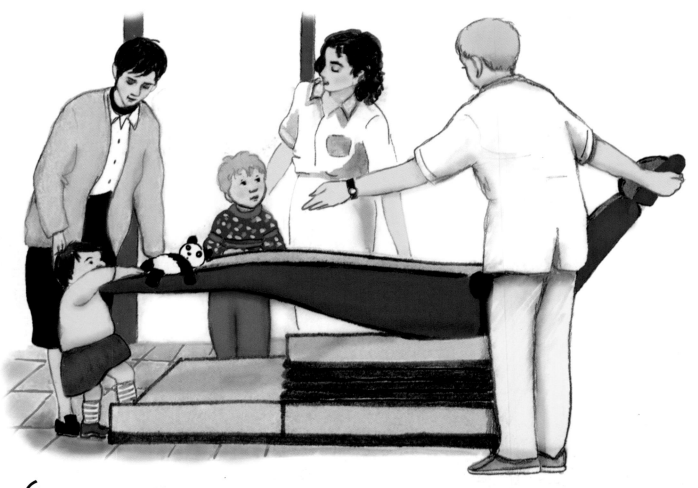

Jenny would rather sit
on Mom's lap.
"Can I count your teeth, Jenny?"

Jenny opens her mouth very wide.
"Nineteen... twenty healthy teeth!"

Clean teeth are
healthy teeth.

7

Sam wants the dentist to count his teeth.
He enjoys riding up and down in the chair.

He looks at all the dials and switches.
Sam feels as though he's in a spaceship.

8

Open wide! The dentist checks
Sam's teeth using a mirror.
The nurse makes a note
about each one.

"This one has a tiny hole.
I'll fill it before it starts to hurt."

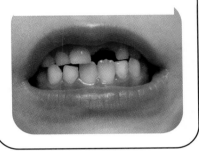

Have you lost
any teeth yet?

One of Sam's teeth looks a bit gray.
"Can you remember knocking this tooth?"
the dentist asks Sam.

Sam remembers. So does Mom.

"An X-ray will show us the new tooth
waiting to replace that gray one.
But I'll do your filling first."

The nurse puts a special bib on Sam.

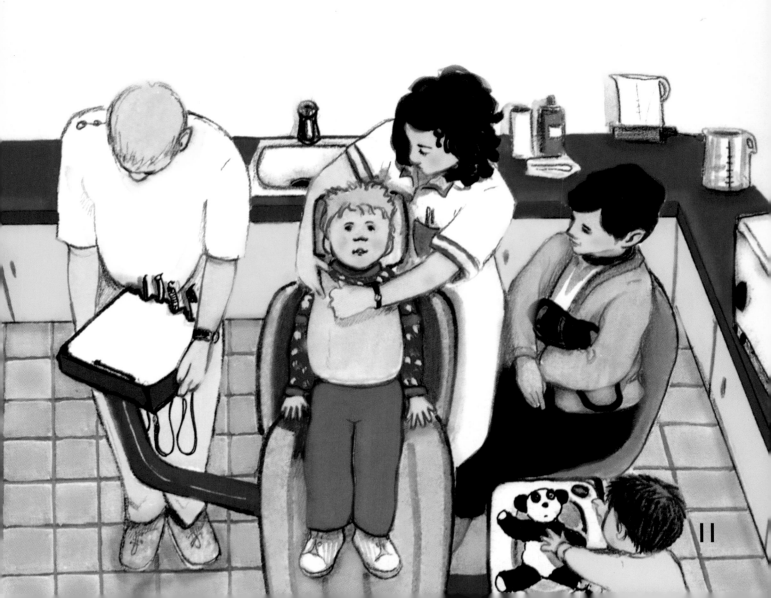

Wheee! The drill makes a whizzing sound.

"This drill will tickle your tooth, Sam, and get the bad bits out." But Sam can't laugh at the tickling with his mouth open.

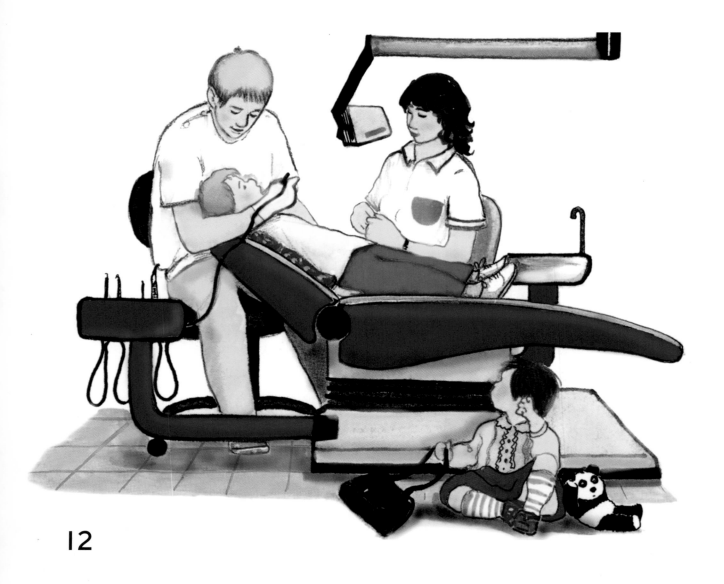

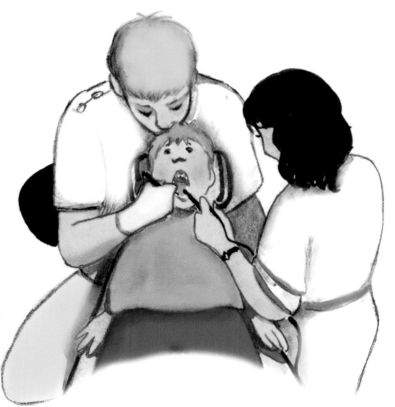

Water comes out of the end of the drill.

The nurse keeps Sam's mouth dry with a tube that sucks the water away.

Then the nurse mixes the filling.

13

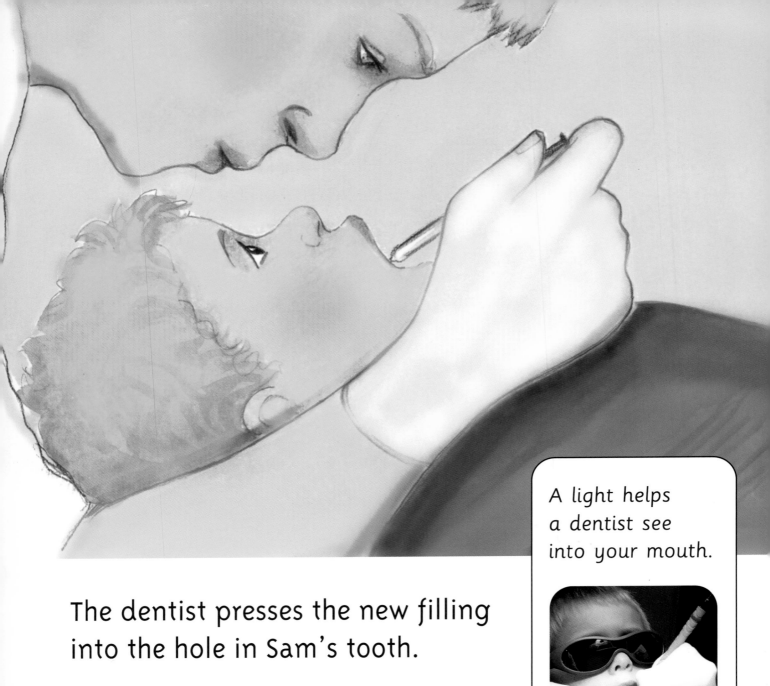

A light helps a dentist see into your mouth.

The dentist presses the new filling into the hole in Sam's tooth.

Scrunch! It makes a funny noise but it doesn't hurt a bit.

14

"Now bite your teeth together, Sam."

Sam's mouth won't shut properly!

The dentist scrapes the filling until Sam's teeth feel right.

"There, all done!"

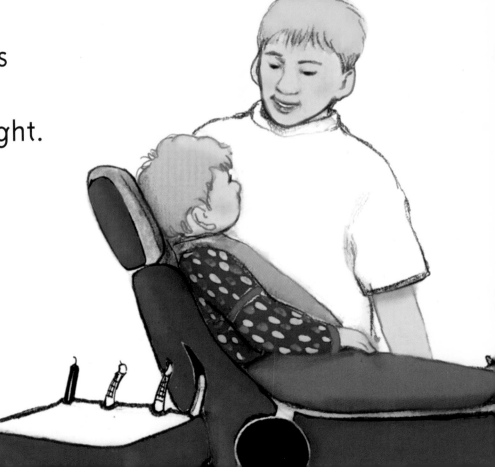

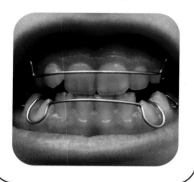

Braces make
teeth straight.

Sam rinses out his mouth
with pink water. It tastes nice.

"Don't swallow it, Sam."
Sam spits out the water.

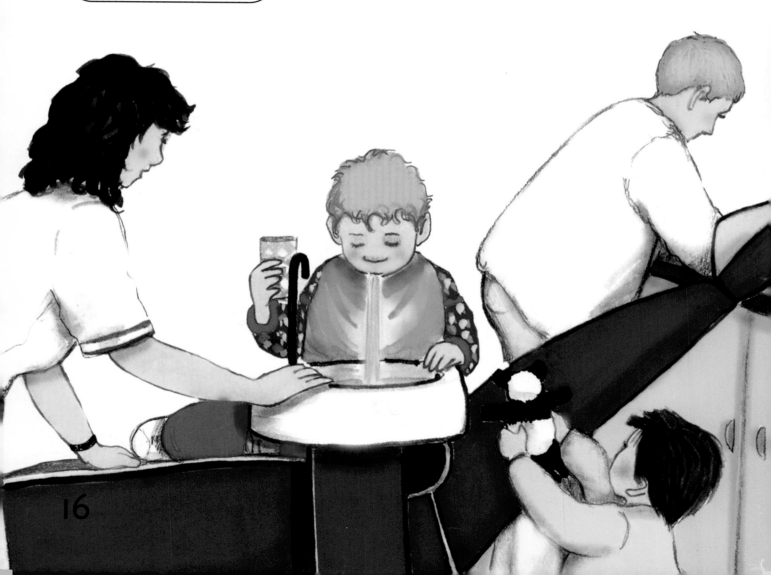

"Open your mouth just once more, Sam."
The dentist polishes Sam's teeth.

The polisher tickles too. When Sam
laughs now his teeth are white and shiny.

Sam wonders what an X-ray feels like.
He bites on a special card
and sits very still.

There! And he didn't feel a thing!

18

"We've taken a picture of your jaw,"
says the dentist.

"You can see the big teeth waiting to
come through. They all look fine to me."

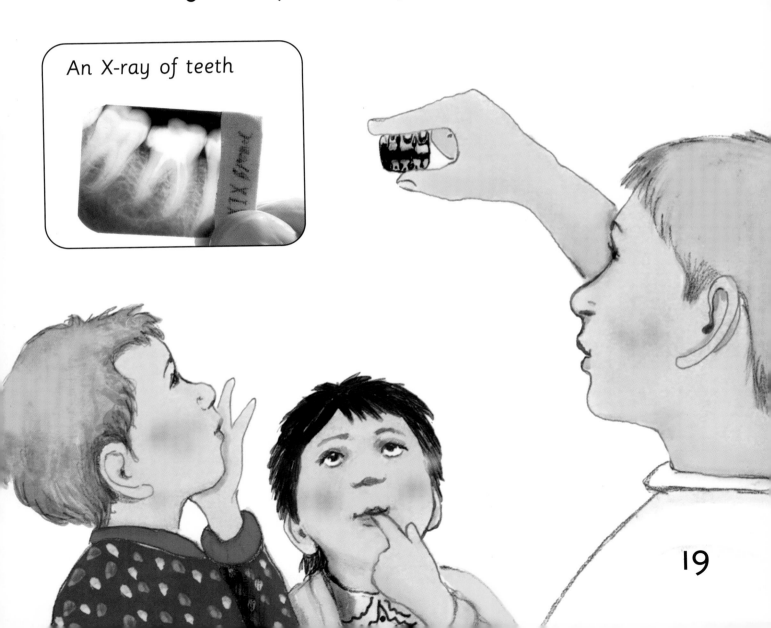

An X-ray of teeth

Sam and Jenny deserve these stickers.
Mom buys new toothbrushes too.

Mom makes an appointment for them
to go back in six months.

"Can we buy some candy now, Mom?"
"No! Jenny has twenty teeth to take
care of and you have your new teeth too!"

So they buy some apples instead.

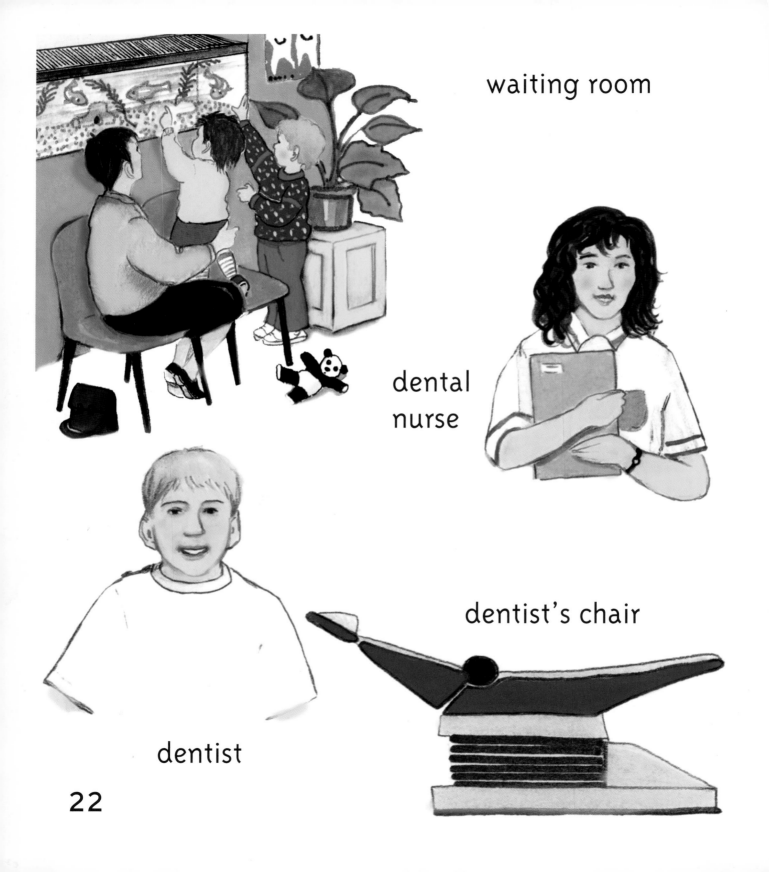

waiting room

dental nurse

dentist's chair

dentist

22

mirror

mouthwash

sticker

X-ray

23

Index

Find out more

Find out more about going to the dentist at:

www.adha.org/kidstuff
www.kidshealth.org
http://familydoctor.org/227.xml
www.oralhealthamerica.org